COMPLICATED COLORING

PRESENTS

COMPLICATED
CHRISTMAS
COLORING

MAGICAL FESTIVE COLORING
FOR KIDS AND GROWN UPS

ILLUSTRATED BY ANTONY BRIGGS

THIS BOOK BELONGS TO

....

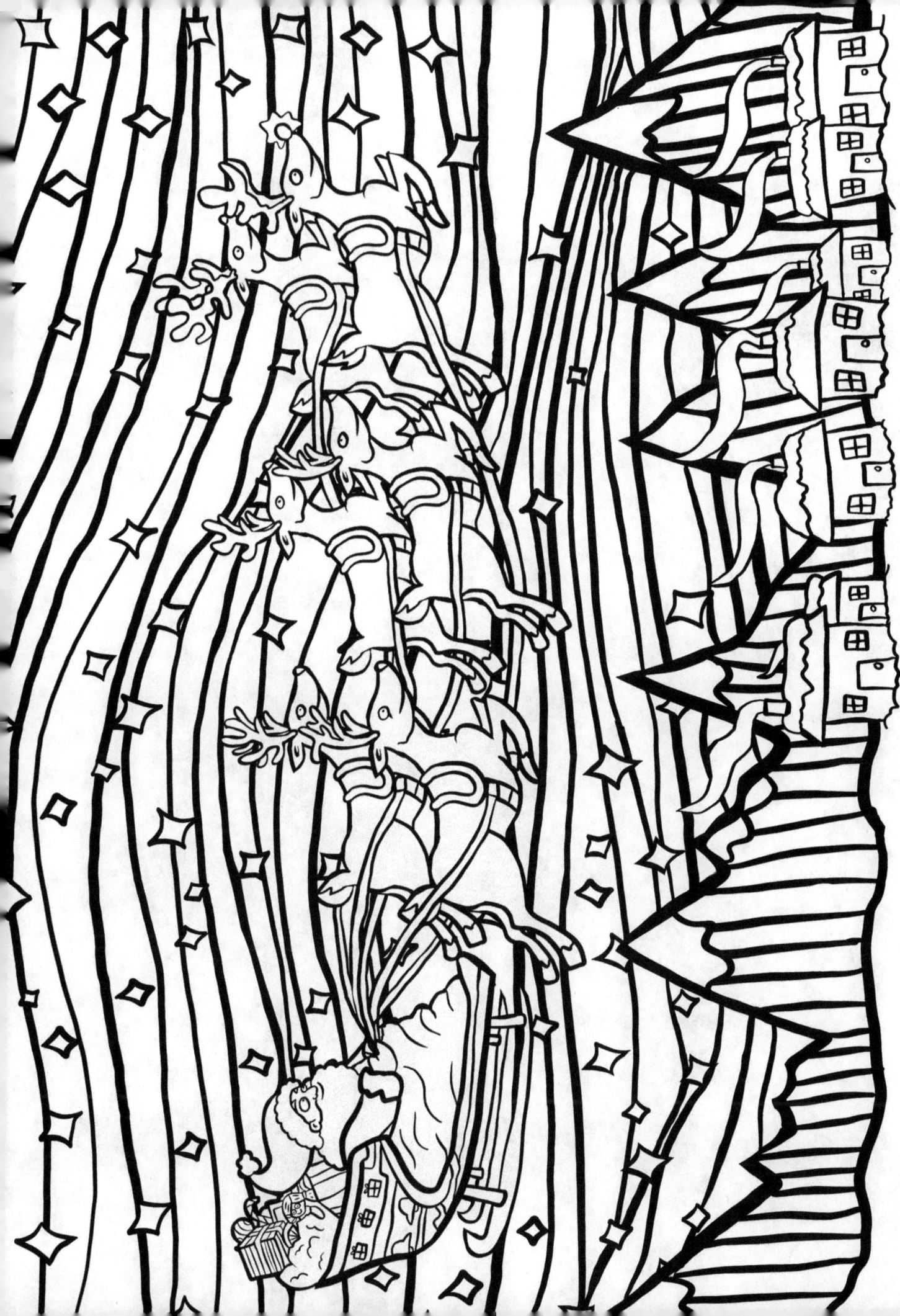

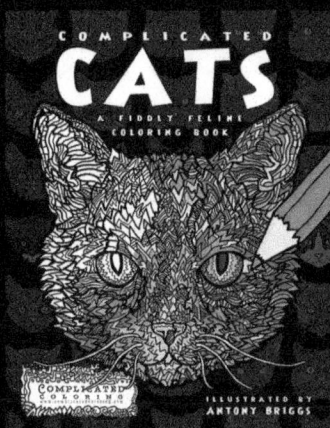

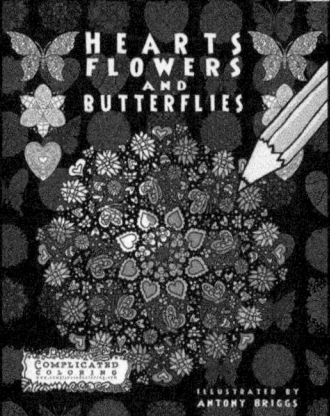

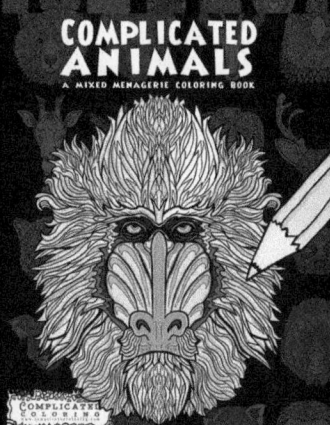

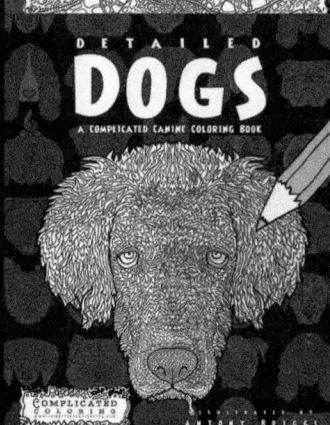

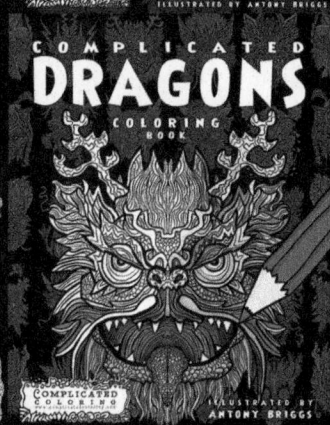

www.ingramcontent.com/pod-product-compliance
Lightning Source LLC
Chambersburg PA
CBHW051351290326
41933CB00043B/3434